Lost & Found

Bri Miller

Presentation by *BookLeaf Publishing*

Web: www.bookleafpub.com

E-mail: info@bookleafpub.com

ISBN: 9789357748650

First edition 2023

To Gage Middleton, who found me, so I could find Myself.

With deepest gratitude & many thanks to:

The Universe, The Cosmos that conspired to not only inspire me throughout my hardships to write my poems, so I could heal my inner world, but also to help me share a bouquet/collection of them in a published form with the World so everyone can have a chance to find a way to go a little deeper.

My Higher Self for the unconditional love, strength & guidance & for always being one step ahead of Me.

My parents, László & Julianna for having me, raising me & understanding me, then slowly trusting me & letting me follow my heart & dreams, so I could grow into the Person I am today. I Love You Both for Eternity.

My Divine Masculine, Gage Middleton: I Thank You 'kindly' for the support, passion & space You've given me ever since our paths have -finally- crossed & for 'the Love I found'.

My Childhood Besties, Betti & Bea for always having my back, celebrating me, cheering me up, listening to me & loving me no matter where I am, what I am doing & who I am becoming! I love you, Girls with all my heart.

My Amazing Friend, Dóra Láving for spoiling me with stories; books; stories about books; books about stories & for cheering me on & walking side by side with me on this journey since the very beginning.

My Soul Sisters, Lucie & Char for all of your wisdom & for sharing a vision & leading with me from the front right from the start.

My Incredible Side-kick, Bree Heacock for being my guardian angel here on Earth in a crazy fun human form.

My Hungarian Companion, Eszter I'Anson for going through hell & back with me & never leaving my side throughout my darkest times.

My two Wonderful professors at Károli Gáspár University: Tibor Fabiny & Katalin G. Kállay for believing in me & trusting me that I would be able to find & unleash my full potential within the English language.

My Acting Coach & Mentor, Jack Scully for helping me harness my emotions & for constantly showing me what is possible.

The English language for opening up the whole wide world for me, for becoming one of my guides, vessels for healing & a huge part of my identity.

My Friends, Family & All the Unique People I have crossed paths with, in any way, shape or form, I Forever Appreciate You for adding to Me & to My Life.

Last but not least, I Thank You, Beautiful Soul, for taking a courageous step towards Your True Self & choosing Me to accompany you even if it is just for a little while; take all the time you need…
-Thank you!

About the Author

Brigitta Molnar (Bri Miller) is a Human Being, Dark Divine Feminine, Daughter, Partner, Friend & Starseed;
She is also a Former Dancer, Gymnast turned into a Holistic Lifestyle Coach & Artist.
She is originally from Budapest, Hungary where she received her BSc degree in English Studies & used it to further her knowledge in the USA as a Personal Trainer, then to heal, transform herself - mind, body & soul- & create her new life both personally & professionally in England where she is now living.

She is currently running her Online Coaching Business as a Holistic Life Coach -specialized in Movements, Lifestyle, Mindfulness - to guide soul-led individuals to Find, Step into & authentically Lead from their True Selves.
She is also in the process of becoming an Actress. And now she is a published author, poet sharing her work about how she lost & then found herself by choosing herself & taking her journey deep within, in her second language.

Lost & Found

I was wondering around
aimlessly; Hearing all the
muffled screaming in my chest
for decades, but not listening

Tears rolling down,
Body's collapsing,
Illness catching up with me,
Mentally in the dark.

I was lost in another self
but all it takes is a person
who not only loves you
but shows you your power:
How you can be found by You.

B.M.

To connect with her find her on
www.bristylecoaching.com
Or instagram.com/bristylecoaching

No Humanity

She switched it off, without alert;
She escaped it & life, as it is;
She did not want to feel the hurt,
She refused to feel the bliss.

She just let herself disappear,
And kept the dark near,
So it would push her to beat
All the life & any kind of fear
Out of her; clear.

She let it hurt her deep,
Let it tear her apart,
Wanted to know in her sleep:
Can she rip out her own heart?

Nothing was left in her,
Nothing, just a blur:
No living poetry,
No humanity;

Only brutality

& pure cruelty.

B.M.

The sound of Your Voice

My own Choice:
Mild and wild,
Made me bright-
Warming and rejoice,
Ashes to the soul.
Grey cover & a hole,
Or Sweet embrace?
Loud and beloved whisper,
Lover of your grace.

When you say I play,
When you shout, I might
fall in love with your Sin,
Your Breath on my skin.
Loving the words that leave your mind.
I don't love you, Are you blind?

No! You want me to abandon
My one and only youth?

I am in love with your expression,
The Fiery Rage of your truth;
All the stories and the mind of yours
That changes, in me, the cycle of wars.

I am not in love with you,
I am in love with your lies.
I am hiding because I just want to rise.
I am not ready to see you,
But I hear you, Dear,
I hear you clear.
I want you, and I want you here.
Next to me, yes, right here.
Your vibrating voice in my ear;
On my mind, I have no fear.

I just love the sound,
'Cause It is our bond;
Utterly beautiful to sing:
'Freedom through wings'.

But how it makes me feel?
I am about to say a great deal:
I am in love,
Herein above:

-

'Melody of your throat,
Vibration of your chords
Resonates with me, lots;
Softness of your breath,
Air and the smell of death;
Song of your expressions,
Tongue-tied confessions;
Anthem of your opinion,
Brush of your articulation;
Sound of your bitter voice,
spelling of your choice;
Divulge my deepest secrets
That makes all the difference,
Gives me no rhyme just confidence.'

-

Say my name!

That's my aim-

In life and death.

Pour out your feelings on me,

Shower me with your vent:

I was sent

To hear you,

To fear you;

Just speak to me!

I can breathe

As you speak to me

'The truth of the World,

The heart of this Earth.'

You make me better,

You make me stronger.

How can I hate you?

But I can't love you.

I keep you here then,

Not close, but when

You are near

My dear,

Anxiety, you are no more,

Not anymore-

that Someone I will Ever interfere.

B.M.

In Stillness

I don't want to hear,
I don't want to feel.

Carried my Self,
Emptied my shelf.

Violently quiet and free
Everything around me.

I am aligned, and truly refined,
Won't ever allow to be defined.

Sitting here speechless,
In this amount of stillness,

Closing my eyes
As the voices rise:

'My sweet, sweet serenity,
Give me back my sanity'.

'Hush now, be silent, My Love'
I fly high, higher than my dearest Dove.

B.M.

Deep-Rest

Laying in bed,

Dizzy in the head.

Depression takes over,

Covers me, he lowers

To whisper in my ear.

Tucks me in, I wear

This warm blanket of dark paradise,

And my chest is paying the price.

I am speechless;

I am sleepless;

I just force my self to feel blessed,

But c'mon; I need to do my best!

I feel, I can't wake up,

my legs & heart feel numb:

I hate the love I receive,

I love the hate I perceive.

But again, I am leading,

I finally am breathing.

That deep-rest leaves my body,
And my depressed mind is free.

B.M

Here I Bow

Allow me to feel,
Then I bow to you to heal,
Looking to release
With peace.
One year and another;
Don't disturb the water!
It might get darker.

Let it be;
Let it be still;
Let it be still now,
& then Here I bow to-

Everything; To fall into place,
Find its own pace:
'Let time heal you
Let them deal with you'.
I'm not here to quit,
I want all the benefit;
Let me go through it.

Through Me-

Through Me to be free-

Through Me to be Free Now;

I want to! I'm here, I Bow!

B.M.

Solitude

The tears made her blind.
She couldn't breathe,
Then she opened her mind:
She began to Create.

B.M.

She Creates

She's focusing so much on the mistakes
She doesn't want to make,
& completely forgets the true happiness
She would be able to create.

B.M.

Supernatural

Feelings are consuming her, completely;
She is dancing on the edge, emotionally;
Warming fire catches her dress, intensely;
But she wants to put it out, immediately.

Love is overflowing her heart, slowly;
Fear is increasing on her mind, blindly;
Passion is bubbling in her veins; Crazy;
She's Supernatural Feelings: Eternally.

B.M.

Once Upon a Time...

He did love her,

but She loved Him more,

& when She fell-

He did not catch her;

He let her go.

B.M.

Broken

The whole journey is yours alone,
to unfold & discover the unknown.

Once the hurt comes with pain,
you'll never ever be the same.

Fragments fallin' off the face of the Old,
Melting pieces into your days of Gold.

Life comes home to you, after being Broken:
Your Mind'll expand & your Eyes'll be wide
Open.

B.M.

Please, Stay

I have abandoned you.
I have wronged you.
I was feeling blue.
I tried to hold myself together like glue.

For her and not for me.
For someone I don't want to be.
Please, leave me to be me.
So I can grow and be free.

I can be me now, I pray:
'I need You to stay,
I wouldn't want it any another way,
So Please, I ask You, to Stay';

How much I've cried;
So many times I've tried,

And Here, I've healed.

Now I am here to be Me; I've stayed.

B.M.

Pain

Embrace it & It'll set you free;
Fight it & it will not even let you

To Be.

B.M.

Her Purpose

She took a deep breath
& smiled,
as she could feel her mind
becoming Wild.
& That moment she sensed:
She's aligned:
She's living That life,
with the view, she designed.

B.M.

Forever Yours

Until you don't choose yourself over others,
You can't be chosen by your Lovers.

B.M.

She Forgave

The One thing: to Forgive;
Can she learn again, to Live?

Falling for Him is the Past;
Now, she really needs to rest.

She will either be freed,
Or she'll sit there & bleed.

The One to Brave, then to Save;
She's no longer her own slave.

Strivin' to become Her best,
Yes; She's here, she's Blessed:

With Her Forgiving deed,
She can & will: Love & Lead.

B.M.

Their Soul Contract

She embraced the unknown;
Like it was Her own.

He embraced the unknown;
Like it was His own.

B.M.

Infinite

We could not let go;
We held until we knew.

The whole wide world
conspired to help us burn;
Pressed our bodies together,
And created us Forever.

There was nothing else; no secret:
In that moment, we were Infinite.

B.M.

Butterflies

This is a brand new start to Feel,
Everything is happening for real.

As soon as your inside starts to Heal,
Your magnificent wings will appear.

B.M.

How They Fly

When His eyes are locking with Hers,
The world they have together, Burns.

Her touch comes to him with passion,
Opening up their feelings like Ocean.

Their true connection is one of a kind,
As they speak the words with open mind:

He sometimes keeps Her off of the sky,
But then She teaches Him how to fly.

B.M.

Because...

I surrender to you,
*L*eaving the old behind.
*O*pening my heart up;
*V*isible only to Your eye.
*E*mbracing the New:
*Y*ou & Me aligned.
*O*ne taste from that cup,
*U*sing Our hearts to fly.

B.M.

Our December

With the last chapter of the Year,
We have created something Real:

Decorated our Souls with Warmth;
Welcoming Us in those Loving arms.

Talked to each others' Inner Worlds,
That finally uncaged our little Birds.

Listened to songs we have Found,
And held one another all Day round.

Preparing us for the End of this Part,
As Our new Beginning is about to Start.

B.M.

I am glad I Found You.

www.ingramcontent.com/pod-product-compliance
Lightning Source LLC
La Vergne TN
LVHW010921200726

843509LV00013B/2026